Snap Happy

Written by Alison Hawes

Illustrated by Mike Phillips

Harcourt
Supplemental Publishers

Rigby • Steck-Vaughn

www.steck-vaughn.com

Anna is my sister.

I am taking pictures on her big day.

Taking pictures makes me happy.

Mr. Flash says, "I love to take pictures.
Taking pictures makes me happy.
I am taking pictures on Anna's big day."

I take a picture of Anna and my dad.
So does Mr. Flash.

4

Anna says, "I am so excited!"

I say, "Even I am excited!"

Mr. Flash does not say anything.

5

I take a picture of Anna and Carlos.
So does Mr. Flash.

6

Carlos says, "I am so happy."

I say, "Even I am happy."

Mr. Flash does not say anything.

Mr. Flash puts his pictures in a book.
When we look at them, I am in them all!

8

Anna says, "I am so sad."

Mr. Flash says, "I am so mad!"

I do not say anything.

Anna and Mom

mom and Dad

Anna and Carlos

Anna and Dad

I put my pictures in a book.

Anna and I look at the pictures.
When we look, Anna says, "I love them!
Your pictures make me so happy!"